Let's Fly
PASSENGER PLANES

by Wendy Hinote Lanier

FOCUS READERS

www.focusreaders.com

Focus Readers is distributed by North Star Editions:
sales@northstareditions.com | 888-417-0195

Produced for Focus Readers by Red Line Editorial.

Photographs ©: Photo_works/Shutterstock Images, cover, 1; Milkovasa/Shutterstock Images, 4–5; DiegoMariottini/Shutterstock Images, 6; Ivan Cholakov/Shutterstock Images, 8–9; Aviation History Collection/Alamy, 11; johnbraid/Shutterstock Images, 13; GRC/NASA, 14–15; Thomas_EyeDesign/iStockphoto, 16–17; Birute Vijeikiene/Shutterstock Images, 19; Vytautas Kielaitis/Shutterstock Images, 21, 29; Rob Wilson/Shutterstock Images, 22–23; Kodda/Shutterstock Images, 25; David Varga/Shutterstock Images, 27

Library of Congress Cataloging-in-Publication Data
Names: Lanier, Wendy Hinote, author.
Title: Passenger planes / by Wendy Hinote Lanier.
Description: Lake Elmo, MN : Focus Readers, [2019] | Series: Let's fly |
    Audience: Grades 4 to 6. | Includes bibliographical references and index.
Identifiers: LCCN 2018031677 (print) | LCCN 2018030377 (ebook) | ISBN
    9781641853408 (hardcover) | ISBN 9781641853989 (pbk.) | ISBN 9781641855143
    (PDF) | ISBN 9781641854566 (ebook)
Subjects: LCSH: Airplanes--Juvenile literature. | Airplanes--Turbofan
    engines--Juvenile literature.
Classification: LCC TL547 .L4224 2019 (ebook) | LCC TL547 (print) | DDC
    629.133/34--dc23
LC record available at https://lccn.loc.gov/2018031677

Printed in the United States of America
Mankato, MN
October, 2018

About the Author

Wendy Hinote Lanier is a native Texan and former elementary teacher who writes and speaks for children and adults on a variety of topics. She is the author of more than 30 books for children and young adults.

TABLE OF CONTENTS

CHAPTER 1

At the Airport 5

CHAPTER 2

Bigger, Faster, Farther 9

 HOW IT WORKS

Turbofan Engines 14

CHAPTER 3

Parts of a Plane 17

CHAPTER 4

Air Travel Today 23

Focus on Passenger Planes • 28
Glossary • 30
To Learn More • 31
Index • 32

AT THE AIRPORT

A family arrives at the airport. It is early morning. But many people are already there. The people will travel all over the world. First, they wait in line to **check** their bags. Then they go through **security**.

 Passenger planes carry people to and from places all over the world.

 To board the plane, passengers walk through a tunnel called a jet bridge.

Next, they find their gate. They wait there until it is time to board the plane.

On the plane, people find their seats. They watch out the windows as luggage is loaded onto the plane. Then it is time for takeoff. The plane zooms down the runway. Soon it lifts off the ground. It flies high above the clouds.

FUN FACT

In the United States, more than two million people travel on airplanes each day.

CHAPTER 2

BIGGER, FASTER, FARTHER

The airplane was invented in 1903. Over the next 30 years, a few small planes carried passengers. Then **airliners** were invented. The Douglas DC-3 was a famous airliner. It carried 21 passengers.

 A Douglas DC-3 made its first flight in 1935.

People could travel faster and farther than ever before. For this reason, the DC-3 is known as the plane that changed the world.

The Boeing 307 appeared in 1940. It was the first passenger plane with a **pressurized** cabin. The plane could fly above the

FUN FACT

The DC-3 could go more than 190 miles per hour (306 km/h). It could fly across North America in 16 hours.

 The Boeing 307 carried 33 passengers and a five-person crew.

clouds. That meant it could avoid bad weather.

In the 1950s, passenger planes began using jet engines. These engines made the planes fly faster.

The DH-106 Comet and Boeing 707 were the first passenger jets. These jets made air travel easier. Companies could fly more people for less money.

FLYING IN COMFORT

Before 1940, airplanes did not fly higher than 10,000 feet (3,050 m). Air above this height has less oxygen. It is harder for people to breathe. Pressurized cabins keep the air inside the plane similar to the air on the ground. That way, the plane can fly high without hurting passengers.

The Boeing 747 was introduced in 1969. It used **turbofan engines**. And it could hold up to 450 people. The 747 became one of the most successful jets ever built. It is still used today.

TURBOFAN ENGINES

Today, most passenger planes have turbofan engines. The engines are inside large tubes. A huge fan sits at the front of each tube. The fan sends air through and around the engine. In passenger planes, the fans send most of the air around the engines. Less air goes through the center. Sending air around the engines cools and quiets them. This helps them use less fuel. It also produces more **thrust**. The air that goes through the engine's center is mixed with fuel and burned. This creates power to drive the fans.

Scientists continue to design better turbofan engines.

CHAPTER 3

PARTS OF A PLANE

Passenger planes come in several sizes. But most planes have the same basic parts. An airplane's body is called the fuselage. The cockpit is at the front of the fuselage. The pilots sit in this area.

 In the cockpit, the pilots work together to fly the plane.

17

The cabin is behind the cockpit. Passengers sit in the cabin.

The wings are the most important part of an airplane. The shape of the wings creates lift. Lift is an upward

WING SHAPE

The back of an airplane wing comes to a sharp edge. The front of the wing is thicker and rounded. The wing's top is curved. Because of this shape, air flowing over the top of the wing creates low air pressure. High pressure under the wing can push the plane up.

 During takeoff, parts called flaps stick out from the back of the wings. Flaps help create more lift.

force. It causes the plane to rise up into the air. At the same time, thrust moves the airplane forward. Most passenger planes use engines to create thrust.

Smaller planes may have only one engine. Large planes have two to four. Most planes use jet engines. But a few use propellers.

The plane's tail provides balance. It is also used to steer the plane. The tail has two parts. One is the horizontal **stabilizer**. This part

FUN FACT

Propeller planes fly lower and slower than jets. But they can land on shorter runways.

PARTS OF A PASSENGER PLANE

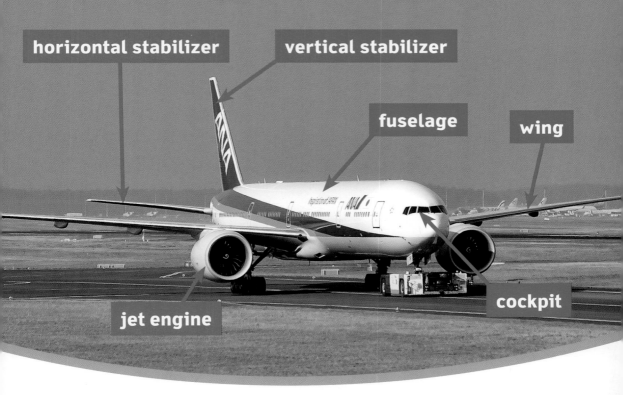

horizontal stabilizer

vertical stabilizer

fuselage

wing

jet engine

cockpit

moves the plane up or down. The other part is the vertical stabilizer. This part moves the plane to the left or right.

CHAPTER 4

AIR TRAVEL TODAY

Millions of people travel on airplanes every day. They can go long distances in just a few hours. Computers help plan the plane's route. Some even help the pilots fly the plane.

 Hartsfield-Jackson Atlanta International Airport in Georgia is one of the busiest airports in the world.

In most planes, the cockpit is the size of a car. That way, the pilots can reach all the controls. The displays are easy to read and use. Every light and switch has a specific purpose. Some tell the pilots about **flight conditions**. Some warn about possible problems.

FUN FACT

A Boeing 747 has 365 switches, dials, and lights in the cockpit.

 Seats in the cabin often have touchscreens on the back.

Airplane cabins must meet safety standards. Seatbelts protect passengers if there is a crash. The cabin also has lights along the floor.

The lights show the way to exit the plane.

Plane crashes are rare. In fact, flying is one of the safest ways to travel. People continue to improve airplanes. They collect information

A GIANT JET

The Airbus A380 is the largest passenger plane in the world. This double-deck plane has two levels of seats. It can carry more than 800 people. Four turbofan engines power the huge plane. It can go more than 9,000 miles (14,500 km) in a single trip.

 An Airbus A380 has a wingspan of 261 feet (80 m).

about many planes and airports.

They study **flight patterns** as well.

This information helps them create

better designs. The new planes

are even safer. They will carry

passengers all over the world.

FOCUS ON
PASSENGER PLANES

Write your answers on a separate piece of paper.

1. Write a sentence describing the key ideas from Chapter 2.

2. Would you rather fly in a passenger plane or travel on a train? Why?

3. Which plane was one of the first passenger jets?
   - A. Airbus A380
   - B. Boeing 707
   - C. Douglas DC-3

4. What would happen if an airplane's wings were not shaped correctly?
   - A. The plane would not have enough lift to fly.
   - B. The plane could not get power from the engines.
   - C. The plane could not hold passengers.

5. What does **gate** mean in this book?

*Next, they find their **gate**. They wait there until it is time to board the plane.*

    A. a part of an airport where people can drop off their bags

    B. a part of an airport where people can get on a plane

    C. a part of a fence that can open and close

6. What does **standards** mean in this book?

*Airplane cabins must meet safety **standards**. Seatbelts protect passengers if there is a crash.*

    A. rules for how an aircraft is built

    B. laws about what jobs people can have

    C. plans to make an aircraft different than usual

Answer key on page 32.

GLOSSARY

airliners
Large, metal airplanes used for carrying passengers.

check
Send bags separately rather than carrying them onto the plane.

flight conditions
Details including the air temperature and weather around an airplane as it flies.

flight patterns
Steps for takeoff, landing, and flight of various aircraft.

pressurized
Brought to an air pressure that is comfortable for breathing.

security
A part of an airport where passengers and their bags are checked to make sure they aren't carrying anything dangerous.

stabilizer
A part of an airplane that the moving parts of the tail are attached to.

thrust
A force that pushes air backward and causes an airplane to move forward.

turbofan engines
Jet engines that use a large fan to help produce more power.

TO LEARN MORE

BOOKS

Amstutz, Lisa J. *Airplanes*. Lake Elmo, MN: Focus Readers, 2017.

Beevor, Lucy. *The Invention of the Airplane*. North Mankato, MN: Capstone Press, 2018.

Harris, Tim. *Superfast Jets: From Fighter Jets to Turbo Jets*. Minneapolis: Hungry Tomato, 2018.

NOTE TO EDUCATORS

Visit **www.focusreaders.com** to find lesson plans, activities, links, and other resources related to this title.

INDEX

A

Airbus A380, 26
airport, 5, 27

B

Boeing 307, 10–11
Boeing 707, 12
Boeing 747, 13, 24

C

cabin, 10, 12, 18, 25
cockpit, 17–18, 21, 24

D

DH-106 Comet, 12
Douglas DC-3, 9–10

F

fuselage, 17, 21

J

jet engines, 11, 20–21

L

lift, 18–19

P

pilots, 17, 23–24

R

runway, 7, 20

S

safety, 25–27
stabilizers, 20–21

T

tail, 20
thrust, 14, 19
turbofan engines, 13,
    14, 26

W

wings, 18, 21